Build an Extreme Green Hot Water Solar Collector

PHILIP RASTOCNY

Publisher: Grasslands Publishing House, 8526 Central Avenue, Brooksville, Florida 34613

ISBN: 0985408111 (English Version)
ISBN: 0985408138 (Spanish Version)

First edition – October, 2010
Second edition – June, 2011
Third edition – March, 2013
Fourth edition – August, 2014

Discover other titles by Philip Rastocny at http://www.Amazon.com

Extreme Green™ is a trademark of Philip Rastocny

Lowe's® and the gable design are registered trademarks of LF, LLC.

El Sid™ is a trademark of Ivan Labs.

Intermatic® is a registered trademark of Intermatic, Inc.

DEDICATION

For all of those struggling do-it-yourself individuals trying to make a
difference and do the right thing for future generations.

.

CONTENTS

LIST OF ILLUSTRATIONS

ACKNOWLEDGMENTS

I wish to thank my wife for her support and kind encouragement, especially when I encountered challenges. I wish to thank my parents for allowing me my own choices, for encouraging my individuality, and for raising my personal awareness to my higher consciousness. And last but not least, I wish to thank the Creator for making this beautiful world in which we live.

Forward

In our current energy crisis, most people are looking for ways to be green and lower their utility usage. These instructions show you how to do just that and setting an example for your friends, neighbors, and especially your family.

These instructions provide you with details on how to build a solar hot water collector that uses no moving parts, requires no electricity for operation, and can work relentlessly for you every day that the sun shines.

A water heater takes a huge chunk out of your utility bill. Typically using 20% to 40% of your monthly bill to operate, your water heater silently drips away at your bank account. Now, you can do something to slow or even stop this drip.

Designed for the weekend do-it-yourselfer, these instructions give you step-by-step solutions to creating a no-moving-parts low-maintenance system that is freeze tolerant and simple to assemble. Requiring minimal skills, almost anyone can do this by him/herself with possibly a little assistance from your talented friends.

Since you use your existing water heater, no electricians are needed. While there are some plumbing, soldering, cutting, screwing, gluing, nailing, caulking, digging, leveling, assembly, etc. skills required these skills are typically used on common DIY projects by average individuals.

A recycled 2-pane glass door is featured in this design that lowers your overall investment and is extremely green for the environment. Using your existing (and still good) conventional water heater – instead of having to buy a new, specifically-designed (and somewhat expensive) hot water solar collector – also keeps your current water heater out of a landfill and keeps more money in your pocket.

So with these thoughts in mind, enjoy yourself while building something that makes a statement not only about your DIY skills but also about your green consciousness. Your friends and family will be amazed at what can be done with things they may see around them every single day. Knowing that you did something that helps the green movement is a fantastic feeling that just cannot beat and you will enjoy hot water heated by the sun for a long time to come.

Take your time, do good work, and have fun.

Philip Rastocny

Disclaimer

> ⚠ **WARNING**: After installing this solar hot water collector into your home hot water system, the water temperature in your water heater will vary widely depending on how much sun is available each day. As a result, **the water temperature in your water heater will not be constant**.
>
> Under certain conditions it is possible for scalding temperatures to be reached inside of the water heater.
>
> To prevent scalding or burns always assure proper cold-water mix before showering, bathing, washing, or exposing skin to hot water.

Every reasonable effort has been made to ensure the accuracy and validity of the information provided in these instructions. However inaccuracies, typographical errors, and incomplete content may still exist.

Some municipalities require building permits and inspections to perform certain aspects of construction beyond the scope of these instructions. Always check with your local building department BEFORE beginning any home project to assure compliance with all regulatory prerequisites.

Introduction

These instructions explain how to build a low-tech, low-cost solar collector that gathers a significant amount of solar energy and easily competes with systems costing hundreds of dollars more. These instructions also use your existing water heater (if it is still good) and other materials readily found in most hardware stores. These instructions explain how to build one 36"x80" solar panel (about 20 square feet of internal heating area) using the glass panel and frame from an exterior sliding glass door.

The National Renewable Energy Laboratory (NREL) recommends about 20 square feet of solar collector for every 40 gallons of water in your water heater for most climates. In central Florida, one of these 20 sq. ft. panels may heat water in a 50 gallon water heater all winter long; in northern climates, the results will be much less. Plan your total collector size based on the size of your present water heater, available sun, and your average temperatures. You can always add more collectors if one proves to not properly heat your water.

I highly recommend you try to locate a used exterior double-pane sliding glass door by posting a want ad on Craig's List or in your local newspaper. Recycling these doors keeps them out of landfills and can be obtained for about 1/10th the price of a new 2-pane glass of this size. New 2-pane glass panels are readily available from any glass retailer if you cannot find one used but a frame is needed to mount the panel on top of the solar collector's frame.

Prerequisites

- This system uses a thermo-siphon principle to operate meaning that there are no moving parts and no electrical power for its operation. This principle requires the top of your solar panel to be LOWER than the bottom of your water heater. Typically, your solar collector will sit about 36" off of the ground. See Part 3 of these instructions to determine exactly how high your solar collector will be.

5

- If there are long pipe runs or inadequate height differentials between the solar collector and the heat exchanger, thermo-siphoning will be inadequate and you will need to supplement flow with pumps (see Appendix C).
- The heat exchanger must always be mounted at the bottom of the water heater.
- Select a location for the solar collector that is as close to your water heater as possible to keep heat loss in the plumbing at a minimum.
- Select a location for your solar collector that gets <u>at least</u> four hours of direct, unobstructed sunlight per day. Remember that to get the absolute maximum amount of heat from the collector, orienting it due south or slightly west of due south is essential.
- You may need a building permit from your county building department when making any changes to your home. If you live in a community with its own restrictions, you may also need approval from that committee. Consult with them before beginning.
- For electric water heaters, make sure that the sacrificial anode is in good condition – otherwise change this anode now before you begin this project.
- If your water heater is old, you may want to replace it now with a more efficient model.
- It's a very good idea to read and understand these instructions before you begin this project. Knowing what's ahead can help you wisely plan your time and resources.
- If you it is not possible to locate your collector in the manner shown in Figure 1, see Appendix C for information on using an electric circulating pump between the collector and the heat exchanger.
- If you live in the Tropics and are certain that there is no chance of your water pipes freezing, see Appendix E.

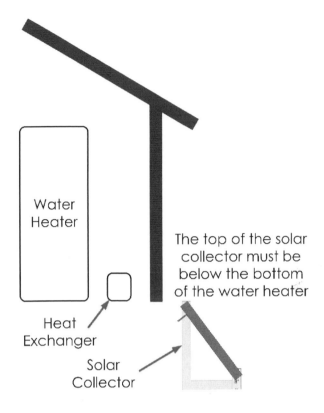

Water
Heater

Heat
Exchanger

The top of the solar
collector must be
below the bottom
of the water heater

Solar
Collector

Figure 1 - Top of Collector must be Below Bottom of Water Heater

Tools

Common hand and power tools are used to fabricate the components and
subassemblies. Most of these tools you probably already own and if not
your neighbor may loan them to you. Rental stores are always at hand to
rent you things you do not want to buy. What you will need:

- Miter saw
- Jig saw
- Circular saw
- Drill
- Pipe cutter
- Sand paper
- Propane torch

- Silver Solder and flux (for potable water use)
- Tape measure
- Carpenter's square
- Marking pencils
- Hole saw (1" drill bit)
- Pipe wrenches
- Crescent wrenches

Materials

The materials needed are broken down into their subassemblies: the water heater, the heat exchanger, the collector, and the ground support frame. All material sizes are based on a collector frame size of 35 ¼" x 78 ¼" (the size of an exterior sliding glass door panel). Appendix A has a complete list of materials with current part numbers and prices from a Lowe's® hardware store.

Water Heater

- Reflectix® insulation – enough to wrap two layers around the side, two layers under the bottom, and three layers around the top
- 2" wide foil tape
- ¾" NPT pipe pieces (fabricated as described later in these instructions)
- Teflon tape

Heat Exchanger

The heat exchanger itself cannot be purchased from a big-box hardware store. See Appendix A for a list of quality manufacturers and order one direct from them. These manufacturers can also provide sizing assistance to assure proper operation.

- 2 gallon (small) expansion tank
- ¾" Female braided connection hoses

- Heat exchanger (30 section minimum)
- Teflon tape
- ¾" Female-to-Female 90 degree elbows
- Reflectix insulation – enough to completely encapsulate the heat exchanger and all interconnecting plumbing
- 2" wide foil tape

Collector (each)

- Double-pane insulated glass (the fixed panel of a 6-foot patio door (36" x 80" panel) works superbly for this and helps recycle materials). This must be standard 2-pane glass (**not the Low-E types**).
- 1"x6" pressure treated wood for the sides (enough to make a perimeter around your glass)
- 4'x8' rolls of Reflectix insulation (enough to insulate all sides and back inside of the collector plus all pipes between the collector and the heat exchanger)
- 4'x8' sheets of foil-backed insulating foam board (enough to insulate all sides and back of the collector)
- 4'x8' sheet of ½" pressure treated plywood
- 2"x2" pressure treated wood for the corner blocks of the frame
- High-temperature flat black engine spray paint
- Wood glue
- Exterior deck screws (stainless steel will last the longest)
- ¾" copper pipe
- ¾" Male-to-Female 90 degree elbows
- ¾" Female-to-Female 90 degree elbows
- ¾" Female pipe-to- ¾" Male threaded adapters
- Exterior window caulk
- 2 ½" exterior deck screws
- Expanding foam insulation
- Reflectix insulation – enough to completely encapsulate the heat exchanger and all interconnecting plumbing
- 2" wide foil tape

- Exterior paint (optional)
- ¼" closed-cell self-adhering foam-rubber seal

Ground Support Frame (each)

- 2'x4'x8' pressure treated wood
- Lag screws
- 3" exterior deck screws
- Concrete Footings
- Exterior paint (optional)

Part 1: The Existing Water Heater

Drain Your Water Heater

1. **Turn off the cold water shutoff valve to the water heater.**
2. Connect a garden hose to the water heater's drain valve.
3. Route the hose downhill to an adequate drain.
4. Open the drain valve.
5. Turn on a nearby hot water faucet to allow air into the water heater.

Examine the Inside of Your Water Heater

Determining the condition of your current water heater is the first step in making a reliable solar hot water system.

1. Using a pipe wrench, remove the drain valve from the water heater.
2. Look inside the water heater through the hole left by removing the drain valve.
3. Check for sediment buildup inside.
   a. If there is sediment buildup, flush clean water through the heater until it is removed. You may need to tip the water heater to get it all out.
   b. If there is rust in the water or the sediment is so built up it cannot be flushed out, **replace the water heater** with a new one.
4. For electric water heaters only, using a pipe wrench remove and examine the anode.
   a. If the anode is mostly dissolved, replace the anode.
   b. If the anode is only partially dissolved you may want to replace the anode now to prevent from having to do it in the future.

Figure 2 - Sediment Flushed from Existing Water Heater

Add Insulation Under Your Water Heater (Electric Models Only)

Note: On the lower electric element, turn the temperature setting down to at least 5 degrees lower than the upper element.

1. Lift the empty water heater off of the ground.
2. Slip two sheets of Reflectix insulation underneath.

Shorten the Cold Water Feed Pipe

1. Disconnect the cold water supply line from the cold water feed pipe.
2. Remove the COLD water feed pipe from the top of the water heater. This pipe is inside of the water heater and is not visible externally.
3. Measure the height of your heat exchanger.
4. Cut off the height of the heat exchanger from the bottom of the feed pipe.
5. Using Teflon tape, re-seal the cold water feed pipe and put it back into the water heater.

6. Tighten the cold water feed pipe being careful not to over tighten.
7. Reconnect the cold water supply line.

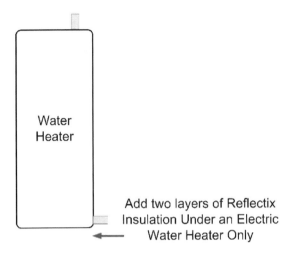

Water Heater

Add two layers of Reflectix Insulation Under an Electric Water Heater Only

Figure 3 - Insulate Under the Water Heater

Install the Heat Exchanger

This process creates a loop from the drain to the cold water inlet and requires custom fabrication depending upon your type of water heater. This is a simple process of cutting and measuring and then using the flex hoses to insert the heat exchanger into the loop. A diagram of this loop is shown below that uses the typical ¾" pipe but your actual pipe size may vary.

Since all water heater installations vary, there is no way to tell you exactly how log and how many pieces of pipe and fittings are needed for your particular installation. Use Male ¾" NPT fittings to connect to the braided flex hoses.

> **Important**: Assemble the loop as shown so that the water will easily flow through smooth bends and whenever possible in a straight line. The fewer the bends there are in this loop, the

greater the water flow will be. This assures
optimal water flow through this loop and
crates as much hot water as possible without
using a pump.

Fabrication of this loop is straight forward. Keep the following in mind:

- The top Tee may need a piece of ¾" pipe to move the external line away from the side of the water heater.
- Make sure that the drain valve can still be operated normally.
- Use Teflon tape on all threaded fittings.
- Allow enough space around pipes and the heat exchanger for future servicing needs.
- Reconnect the cold water line to the water heater (pipe at the top Tee).
- Keep the protective caps over the unused ports of the heat exchanger until Part 4 of these instructions to keep dirt and bugs out.

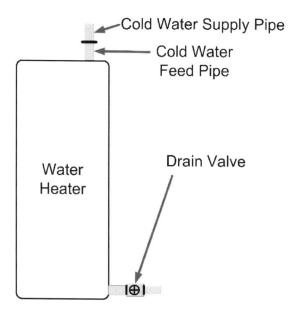

Figure 4 - Pipe Configuration Before

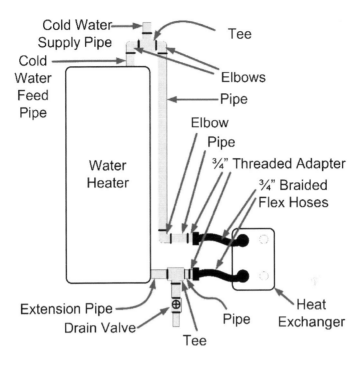

Figure 5 - Pipe Configuration After

Check for Leaks

1. Turn off the water faucet you did earlier in this part.
2. Turn on the main water supply and check your work for leaks.
3. Wait at least 30 minutes to see if there are any slow drips.
4. Tighten or repair leaks as needed.

Insulate the Water Heater and Heat Exchanger

Once you are certain that there are no leaks, insulate the water heater and the heat exchanger with the Reflectix insulation. Wrap at least two layers around the sides and tape all seams with the foil tape. Cut out circular pieces to put on the top and tape all seams with the foil tape. Make sure that there is access to electrical connections and heating element access panels.

> ⚠ **WARNING**: Make sure that proper spacing of this insulation is maintained around all exhaust vents and flues. Check with your local building department for proper spacing requirements and any insulation limitations on your gas or electric water heater.
>
> Improper insulation installation may result in an unsafe operating condition and can result in a fire hazard.

Insulate the hot and cold pipes. Take your time insulating these pipes. Cut the insulation to wrap evenly around the pipes with adequate overlap. Wrap straight sections first and then wrap elbows. Tape all seams with foil tape thereby completely encapsulating the insulation and pipe.

Secure the Heat Exchanger

Secure the heat exchanger in some manner to make sure that it does not move from its place. Metal straps or pipe hangers are good to use in this case.

Insulate All Pipes

Use the Reflectix insulation and wrap all other pipes with at least two layers. Use the foil tape to tape up all seams.

Part 1 Summary

The first step in installing your DIY solar hot water collector is to install the heat exchanger to your existing water heater. Simply adding a bypass loop from the drain to the cold-water inlet provides a non-consumption path into the water stored inside the tank. Using smooth bends and straight pipe sections wherever possible, thermo-sphon (convection) heated water circulates through the bottom-located heat exchanger and into the water heater without the use of any pumps.

The diagram at the right shows the completed installation and the operation of the convection principle.

Convection heating is silent and highly efficient but also a slow process. Similar convection heating is applied to the other side of the heat exchanger later in these instructions providing a totally free heating source.

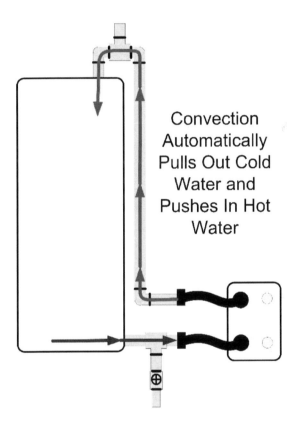

Convection Automatically Pulls Out Cold Water and Pushes In Hot Water

Figure 6 - How Convection Heats the Water Inside the Tank

PHILIP RASTOCNY

Part 2 – Build the Solar Panel

Earlier you selected a location for your solar collector that would orient it in a sunny location and position it so that the top of the solar collector was below the bottom of the hot water tank. You also selected this location so that the pipes running between the collector and the heat exchanger were as short as they could be. Now it's time to build the solar collector panel from the glass and materials you've assembled.

Measure the Glass Frame

Measure the outside of the standard-grade (**NOT LOW-E**) glass panel as shown next:

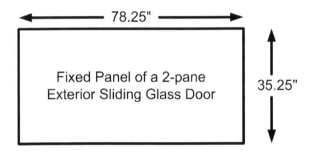

Figure 7 - Dual Pane Glass Panel Dimensions

Cut Out and Assemble the Frame

Measure the length and width to the end of the frame (not to the end of the supports). In the panel I used, the frame measured 78 ¼" long by 35 ¼" wide and the overall dimensions of the panel including the supports was 80" long by 36" wide.

1. Cut out pieces of the 1x6 pressure treated lumber using the miter saw to the lengths you measured.
2. Cut 2x2" pressure-treated corner blocks.
3. Temporarily screw the corner blocks in place.

4. Set the wooden frame onto the door panel and check it for proper fit.
5. Once proper fit is achieved, glue and screw the corner blocks into place.
6. Set the frame on the ½" pressure treated plywood.
7. Trace the frame onto the plywood.
8. Using a power saw, cut out the plywood.
9. Run a bead of waterproof glue around the edge of the frame.
10. Set the plywood piece onto the frame and screw into place using the exterior deck screws.

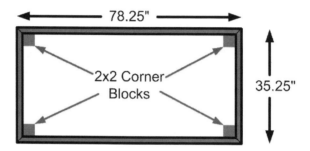

Figure 8 - Match Frame Dimensions to Dual Pane Dimensions

Install the Bottom Insulation

Two layers of insulation are needed in the interior of the collector frame: first a layer of Reflectix insulation rests against the pressure treated wood and then this is covered with a layer of Foil Foam Insulation with the shiny side facing out. The shiny side works like a mirror to reflect sun back to the pipes.

1. Cut out the Reflectix insulation to lie in the bottom.
2. Staple into place.
3. Cut out the Foil Foam Insulation Board to lie in the bottom.
4. Use foil tape to tape lightly into place.

Install the Internal Supports

1. Cut out three pieces of 2x2 pressure treated wood 33 ¾" long to fit just inside the width of the frame.
2. Install the supports in the bottom of the frame (resting on the bottom Foil Foam Insulation) as shown below.
3. Using one exterior deck screw on each end of each support, screw in through the sides of the frame.
4. Use foil tape and cover the exposed side surfaces (not the top) of the internal supports to add reflectivity to these supports.

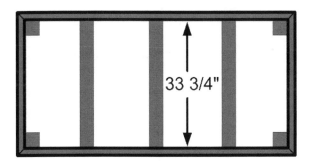

Figure 9 - Add Equally Spaced Internal Supports

Install the Side Insulation

Two layers of insulation are needed in the interior of the collector frame: first a layer of Reflectix insulation rests against the pressure treated wood and then this is covered with a layer of Foil Foam Insulation with the shiny side facing out. The shiny side works like a mirror to reflect sun back to the pipes.

1. Cut out the Reflectix insulation to fit along the four sides of the frame. Notch the insulation to fit around the internal supports.
2. Staple into place.
3. Cut out the Foil Foam Insulation Board to fit the wooden frame sides. Notch the insulation to fit around the internal supports.
4. Glue lightly into place.

5. Use metal tape to tape the seams between the side and bottom insulation boards.
6. Use one long strip of foil tape along the top of the insulation boards to the top of the frame (all four sides).

Solder the Elbows Together

Using the propane touch and silver solder, solder a Female-to-Female elbow into a Male-to-Female elbow.

1. Sand the ends of all pieces (inside and out) where they touch and will be soldered together.
2. Wipe solder flux to the inside and outside of the pieces where they will be soldered (outside on the male end and inside on the female end).
3. Put one M-F elbow into one F-F elbow.
4. Stand the two pieces up on end on a flat surface to assure square alignment (see below).

   NOTE: Take your time at this point to do this properly since small misalignments here make big differences in how flat the total assembly will lay. Test how flat they are by trying to rock the assembly with your finger from the joint. When they are flat they will not rock.
5. Using the propane torch and silver solder, solder the connection.
6. Repeat for 17 total elbow U-assemblies.

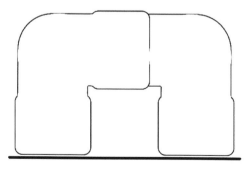

Figure 10 - Properly Soldered U-Assembly

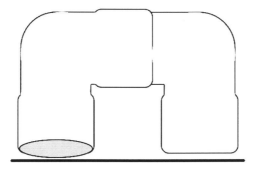

Figure 11 - Improperly Soldered U-Assembly

Cut the Straight Copper Pipe Pieces

The copper pipe zigzags back and forth inside the collector frame and is suspended by the three 2x2 supports above the Foam Foil insulation on the back panel. This permits the sunlight to reach all sides of the pipe rather than just the sun side thereby increasing collection efficiency.

1. Measure the interior width dimension between the Foam Foil insulation (should be about 74").
2. Subtract 4" from this width.
3. Cut 11 pieces of the copper tubing to this value (should be about 68").
4. Cut one piece 2½" longer than this value (should be about 70 ½").

Solder the U-Assemblies to the Straight Pipe

NOTE: The first and last ends of the zigzag pipe do not have U-connections on them.

1. Sand the ends of all pieces (inside and out) where they touch and will be soldered together.

2. Wipe solder flux to the inside and outside of the pieces where they will be soldered (outside on the male end and inside on the female end).
3. Put the straight pipe lengths into the U-assemblies as shown below.
4. Put the 2½" longer piece at the end of the assembly (row 12).
5. Lay them on a flat surface like a concrete driveway.

   NOTE: Take your time at this point to do this properly since small misalignments here make big differences in how flat the total assembly will lay. It is important to get this as flat as possible.
6. Using the propane torch and silver solder, solder each connection.

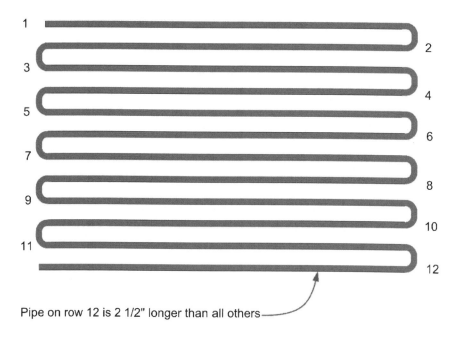

Pipe on row 12 is 2 1/2" longer than all others

Figure 12 - First Step of Zigzag Assembly

⚠ **Caution:** Now that the assembly is soldered together, twist it as little as possible. Applying twists and stresses to the joints while lifting or moving the zigzag assembly can cause it to leak.

Add the Return Plumbing

1. Put a F-F elbow on the 2" longer piece at the end of the assembly (row 12).
2. Cut a piece of straight tubing 23" long.
3. Sand the ends of all pieces (inside and out) where they touch and will be soldered together.
4. Wipe solder flux to the inside and outside of the pieces where they will be soldered (outside on the male end and inside on the female end).
5. Solder all joints.

At this point the whole zigzag assembly should lay completely flat and look something like what is shown below.

Figure 13 - Second Step of Zigzag Assembly

Test Fit the Assembly in the Frame

With the frame lying flat on the ground, test fit the assembly in the frame as shown below. Make sure that there is enough room on the left side to allow additional pipe connections without touching the frame on the right side. The whole zigzag assembly should fit flat on the three internal supports as shown below. Small deviations are tolerable but if the assembly is severely misaligned they must be straightened and re-soldered.

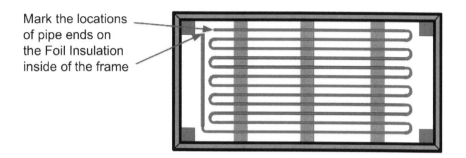

Mark the locations of pipe ends on the Foil Insulation inside of the frame

Figure 14 - Test Fitting the Zigzag Assembly in the Frame

With the zigzag assembly set in place to its final position, use a permanent writer to mark the position of the end of the row 1 pipe and the end of the return pipe on the insulating foam foil inside the bottom of the frame. You will use these marks later in cutting out the exit hole through the back of the frame.

Add the Mounting Brackets

The zigzag pipes will expand and contract inside of the collector every day. Alternate rows on the left side of the zigzag assembly are fixed with mounting brackets to the supports to anchor them properly in place.

1. With the zigzag assembly in its final position, place one ¾" copper mounting bracket onto row 1 centered on the wooden internal support.
2. Temporarily screw down this bracket.
3. One by one, add brackets to rows 3, 5, 7, 9, 11, and 12 of the zigzag assembly.
4. Solder the point where the brackets touch the zigzag assembly.
5. Solder them all securely in place.
6. Remove the temporary screws from bracket 1.

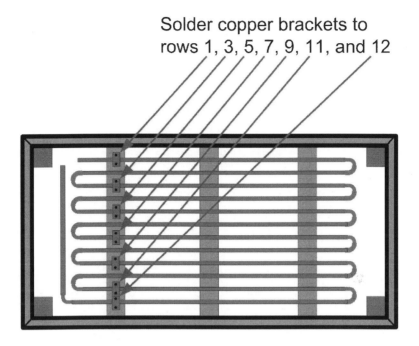

Solder copper brackets to rows 1, 3, 5, 7, 9, 11, and 12

Figure 15 - Solder Fixed Mounting Brackets on Every Other Row

Cut an Exit Hole in the Frame

1. Remove the zigzag assembly from the frame and place it upside down on the same surface you soldered the U-assemblies.
2. Raise the frame off of the ground (tip against a wall or place on top of blocks).
3. From the inside of the frame, use the marks noting the row 1 and the return pipes and draw an oval at least 1 ½" larger than the marks on the foil.
4. Drill a pilot hole inside the oval for the saw bit and then use a jig saw to cut out the exit hole.

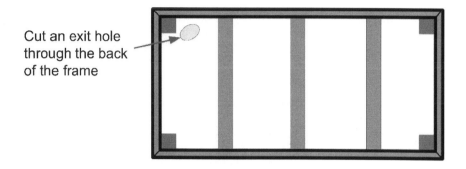

Cut an exit hole through the back of the frame

Figure 16 - Cut an Exit Hole in the Frame

Make Two Exit Stubs

1. Cut two pieces of straight pipe 6" long.
2. To one F-F elbow, add one of the 6" pipes.
3. Sand the ends of all pieces (inside and out) where they touch and will be soldered together.
4. Wipe solder flux to the inside and outside of the pieces where they will be soldered (outside on the male end and inside on the female end).
5. Solder the joint.

Figure 17 - Exit Stub

Make Two Adapters

1. Cut two pieces of straight pipe 3" long.
2. To one F-F 45 degree elbow, add one of the 3" pipes.
3. On the other end of the 3" pipe, add a ¾" threaded adapter.

28

4. Sand the ends of all pieces (inside and out) where they touch and will be soldered together.
5. Wipe solder flux to the inside and outside of the pieces where they will be soldered (outside on the male end and inside on the female end).
6. Solder the joints.

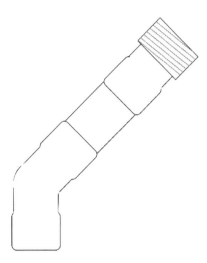

Figure 18 - Slip-to-Threaded Adapter Piece

Add the Exit Stubs to the Zigzag Assembly

1. Make sure the zigzag assembly is upside down.
2. Add an exit stub to the open ends of zigzag tubes.
3. Point the exit stubs vertical (straight up) and parallel to each other.
4. Sand the ends of all pieces (inside and out) where they touch and will be soldered together.
5. Wipe solder flux to the inside and outside of the pieces where they will be soldered (outside on the male end and inside on the female end).
6. Solder all joints.

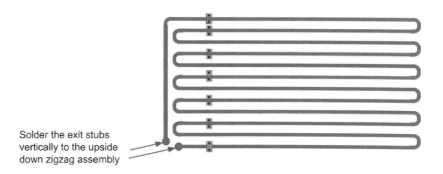

Solder the exit stubs
vertically to the upside
down zigzag assembly

Figure 19 - Add Exit Stubs to Zigzag Assembly

Add the Threaded Fitting Adapters to the Exit Stubs

1. Add both threaded fitting adapters to the open ends of exit stubs.
2. Point the adapters to the top of the frame (as shown below) and parallel to each other. Make sure that the spacing between the two threaded heads allows you to screw on the flex hoses without obstruction. (These adapters can be bent by hand later as long as they are reasonably spaced now.)
3. Sand the ends of all pieces (inside and out) where they touch and will be soldered together.
4. Wipe solder flux to the inside and outside of the pieces where they will be soldered (outside on the male end and inside on the female end).
5. Solder all joints.

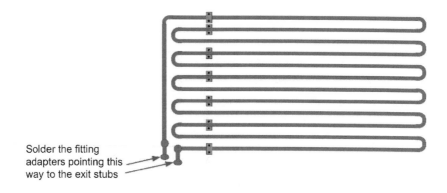

Solder the fitting
adapters pointing this
way to the exit stubs

Figure 20 - Adding Slip-to-Threaded Adapter Pieces to Exit Stubs

Pressure Test the Zigzag Assembly

1. With the zigzag assembly still upside down, gently slide two 2"x4" boards under the assembly so that you can see the bottom of all soldered joints.
2. Connect both flex hoses to the assembly.
3. Connect a garden hose to one of the flex hoses.
4. Connect the garden hose to a water spigot.
5. Slowly turn on the hose and let the entire assembly fill with water. Let water run out of the open flex hose until there is no air coming out (still running in a slow stream).
6. Turn off the water.
7. Put the ¾" plug in the end of the other flex hose.
8. Turn the water back FULL ON.
9. Wait for at least 30 minutes and check for leaks. If leaks are found, drain the assembly and repair the leaks by re-soldering the joint. Repeat this water test until all leaks are fixed.

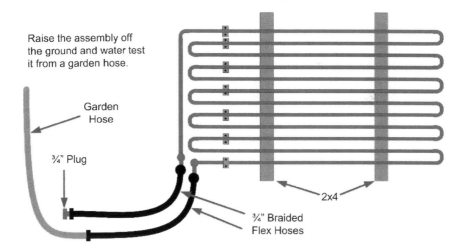

Figure 21 - Pressure Test Zigzag Assembly

Drain the Zigzag Assembly

1. Once the assembly is leak free, remove the braided flex hoses.
2. Tip the return line toward the ground.

3. Slowly rotate the entire assembly clockwise (as seen in the picture above) at least 20 times to drain out the water from the pipes.
4. Once the water stops draining out, **blow into one end to be certain that all water is out** (air should flow freely through the assembly).
5. If it does not, either continue rotating or blow the line out with a pressure hose (blower side of a vacuum cleaner or higher pressure air source).

Small amounts of water will remain trapped inside. Get as much water out of the assembly as possible before proceeding.

Paint the Zigzag Assembly

1. Suspend the zigzag assembly in some manner so that you can reach both the front and back sides without touching the assembly. One method to do this is to temporarily erect a very high workhorse from 2x4s using a workhorse bracket set available from your local hardware store.
2. Use coat hangers to loop through the holes of the copper brackets so that the assembly hangs securely and only touches the assembly at two points.
3. Tape off the threads on the adapter ends with painter's tape so that they will not be painted in this process.
4. Wipe down all surfaces of the zigzag assembly with acetone to remove any grease and remaining flux.
5. Using the high-temperature flat black engine paint, spray one light coat of paint on all surfaces of the assembly, both front and back (including the mounting brackets).
6. Wait for this coat to completely dry (typically one hour).
7. Move the hangers a little to one side to expose the unpainted area.
8. Spray a second coat on all surfaces of the assembly.
9. Allow this coat to dry (typically two hours).
10. Remove the painter's tape.

Install the Oak Glides and Rubber Seal in the Frame

1. Cut three pieces of 2" x ¼" oak panels 31 1/8" long (same size as the supports).
2. Glue and screw down these glides on the supports.
3. Add the closed-cell weather stripping around the top edge of the frame.

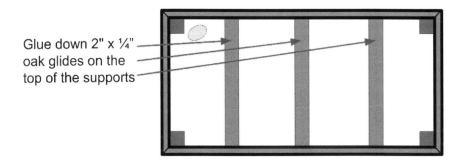

Glue down 2" x ¼" oak glides on the top of the supports

Figure 22 - Glue Oak Glides to Zigzag Supports (One Each)

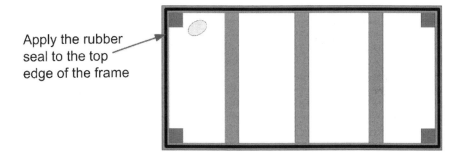

Apply the rubber seal to the top edge of the frame

Figure 23 - Seal Perimeter of Frame

Install the Zigzag Assembly in the Frame

1. Prop up the fame.
2. Once the assembly is thoroughly dry, carefully slide the exit stubs through the exit hole in the back of the frame.
3. Center the brackets on the supports.

4. Using the exterior deck screws, screw the brackets into the support.

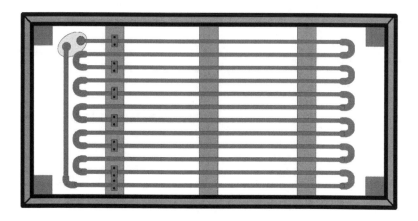

Figure 24 - Screw Zigzag Frame to Oak Glide

Install the Top Glides

1. Cut two pieces of 1"x2" oak board 31" long.
2. Lay the boards on top of the zigzag pipe at the middle and right glides and mark the location of the pipes where they touch the board.
3. Cut a 1" hole in the center of the board at every mark.
4. Trim the bottom of the boards just to the hole.
5. Using a jig saw, cut straight notches into the holes so that this board will fit on top of the zigzag pipes.
6. Drill a hole big enough between these holes so the exterior deck screws will slide through them.
7. Screw the boards over the zigzag pipes.

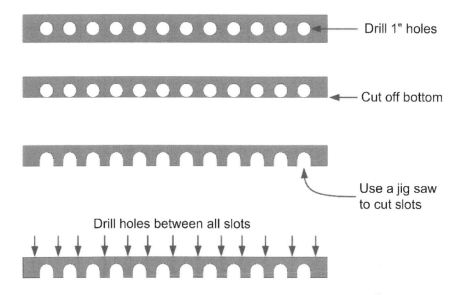

Drill 1" holes

Cut off bottom

Use a jig saw
to cut slots

Drill holes between all slots

Figure 25 - Cutting Out the Top Oak Glides

Install the Glass Panel on the Frame

These instructions assume that you are using the fixed panel of a 6-foot sliding glass door with frame. If you are using a dual-pane glass panel without a frame, you must also build a frame for the glass (not described herein) to emulate that of a fixed panel patio door.

1. Clean both sides of the glass pane with a quality glass cleaner.
2. With the frame still propped up, set the glass panel on top of the frame. Use the long edge of the glass frame to overlap the top of the solar frame.
3. Shift the glass panel so that the glass frame is square on top of the solar frame.
4. Use the exterior deck screws to attach the frame into place. Carefully screw through the metal glass frame from the top and face.

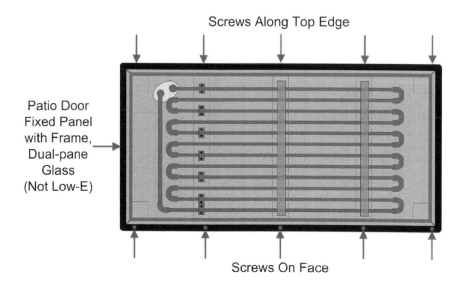

Figure 26 - Install the Dual-Pane Glass on the Frame

Dry Out the Zigzag Assembly

1. Orient the frame so that it is facing the sun head on. Prop it up against your house or a sturdy fence to protect the exit tubes.
2. Keep additional moisture (rain, dew, etc.) from entering the zigzag assembly while drying by covering the exit tubes but not blocking them off.
3. Allow the sun to heat the remaining water in the zigzag assembly and dry it out completely.

NOTE: This drying process may take a few days to get the zigzag assembly completely dry. While it is drying, you should notice at some point steam escaping from the tubes. Once this steam stops, continue drying the assembly for one more full day.

Part 2 Summary

The second step in installing your DIY solar hot water collector is to build the solar collector panel. A wooden frame holds black-painted copper tubes that zigzag back and forth inside to gather sunlight energy and transfer this energy to the heat exchanger installed in Step 1. The fixed panel from a double-pane exterior sliding glass door provides an ecologically sound way of recycling while lowering your carbon footprint.

Two different kinds of insulation inside the frame keep heat inside; the reflective surface of the foil insulation also heats the underside of the zigzag pipe assembly.

Drying out the water from inside the copper tubes is essential to prevent freezing of this assembly during long cold nights in winter cold snaps.

Glides inside the collector allow the zigzag assembly to expand and contract without deforming the pipes and jeopardizing the integrity of the solder joints.

PHILIP RASTOCNY

Part 3 – Build the Support Frame

By now you have installed the heat exchanger on your water heater and assembled the solar collector frame. While the water is drying out of the zigzag assembly, you can build the support frame to permanently aim the collector at the appropriate angle to the sun.

Traditional wisdom states using the same angle as your latitude for the angle of your solar collector; I recommend against that. Solar collectors work best in the summer when the ambient temperature is closer to the desired water temperature. Unfortunately, in winter there are fewer hours of daylight so the amount of time needed to heat water in the winter is also shortened.

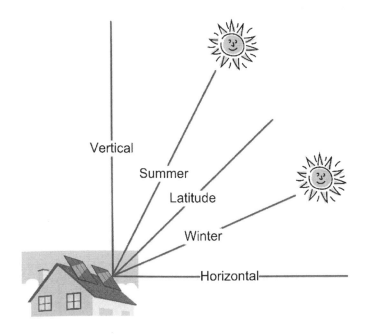

Figure 27 - Sun's Position in Summer and Winter

I recommend using a modified version of your latitude to decrease efficiency in the summer and increase your efficiency in winter. To do this, simply **multiply your latitude by 1.3** to tip the collector slightly more toward the sun in the winter. Below is an example of how to determine the proper angle for optimal winter performance.

Location: Tampa Florida

Latitude is 28.3° N. or about 28°

Tilt Angle is the Latitude * 1.3 = 28 * 1.3 or about 37°

So in Tampa, you would tilt your solar collector about 37 degrees as measured with a digital level on the surface of the glass surface of your solar collector to obtain higher solar performance in the weeks around December 23 and lower solar performance in the weeks around June 23.

Determine your Latitude

1. Find the latitude of your home. You can find this out from your local post office or by searching for the word "latitude" on the internet.
2. Round your latitude off to the nearest whole degree.
3. Multiply this value by 1.3 to know your Tilt Angle. (The Tilt Angle is the number of degrees you will see when placing a digital level on the glass surface of your solar collector).

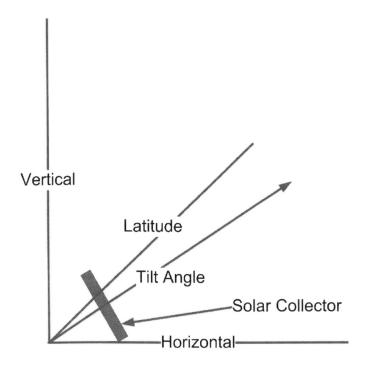

Figure 28 - Determine Your Latitude and Tilt Angle

Write these numbers down here:

LATITUDE = _____ degrees

TILT ANGLE = _____ degrees

Support Board Lengths

The table below assumes that the panel of the solar collector frame is
35.25"x78.25". Use this table to determine the length of the support
boards for the frame of your solar collector. Note that the sizes of these
boards take into account any extra lengths needed for board overlap.

Latitude	Tilt Angle	Board A	Board B	Board C	Board D
0	5	9.0	38.7	8	75.25
2	5	9.0	38.7	8	75.25
4	5	9.0	38.7	8	75.25
6	8	10.1	38.6	8	75.25
8	10	11.1	38.5	8	75.25
10	13	12.1	38.4	8	75.25
12	16	13.1	38.2	8	75.25
14	18	14.1	38.0	8	75.25
16	21	15.1	37.8	8	75.25
18	23	16.1	37.6	8	75.25
20	26	17.0	37.3	8	75.25
22	29	18.0	37.0	8	75.25
24	31	19.0	36.7	8	75.25
26	34	35.6	24.1	8	75.25
28	36	36.2	23.3	8	75.25
30	39	36.7	22.4	8	75.25
32	42	37.3	21.6	8	75.25
34	44	37.8	20.7	8	75.25
36	47	38.3	19.8	8	75.25
38	49	38.7	18.9	8	75.25
40	52	39.2	17.9	8	75.25
42	55	39.6	17.0	8	75.25
44	57	39.9	16.1	8	75.25
46	60	40.3	15.1	8	75.25

Latitude	Tilt Angle	Board A	Board B	Board C	Board D
48	62	40.6	14.1	8	75.25
50	65	40.9	13.2	8	75.25
52	68	41.2	12.2	8	75.25
54	70	41.4	11.2	8	75.25
56	73	41.6	10.2	8	75.25
58	75	41.8	9.2	8	75.25
60	78	41.9	8.2	8	75.25

Figure 29 - Board Length Table

Although the values in the above table are exact, you can round them off to the nearest quarter inch for acceptable results.

1. Cut two boards to length A.
2. Cut two boards to length B.
3. Cut two boards to length C.
4. Cut two boards to length D.

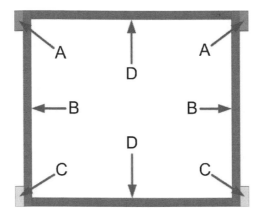

Figure 30 - Support Frame, Top View (not to scale)

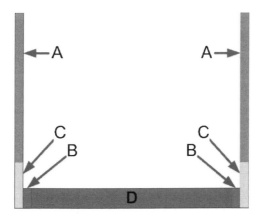

Figure 31 - Support Frame, Front View (not to scale)

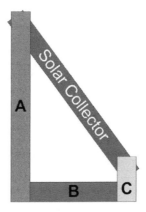

Figure 32 - Support Frame, Side View (not to scale)

Notch the Boards

Cut a 1 ½" high and ¾" deep notch in one end of pieces A and C.

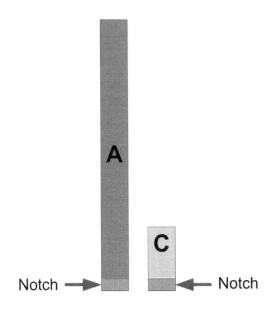

Figure 33 - Board Notches, Front View

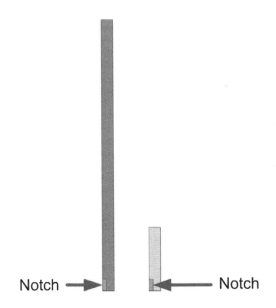

Figure 34 - Board Notches, Side View

Assemble the Frame

1. Assemble pieces D and B.
2. Screw 3" exterior deck screws in from the side (4 places).

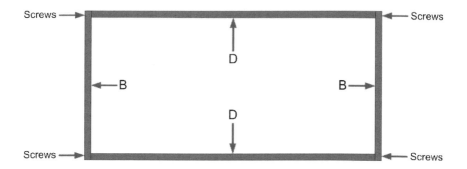

Figure 35 - Assemble Frame

3. Add pieces A and C (notched sides down and out).
4. Screw 3" exterior deck screws in from the side (4 places).

Figure 36 - Add Frame Supports

Assemble the Footings

The footings used in these instructions are the preformed x-slot style typically used with decks and stairs. The slot accommodates 2x4s and 4x4s less any anchoring.

Note: Concrete filled 24" deep and 6" diameter Sonotubes with rebar and J-bolts may be required in some locations. Always check with your building department to assure properly designed footings.

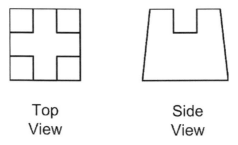

Top   Side
View   View

Figure 37 - Slotted Footings

To properly secure the collector frame to the footing, a simple L-anchor must be attached to this footing. Simply drill a 3/8" hole in the center of the footing and insert a weatherproof 3/8" carriage bolt, washer, and nut to secure the L-bracket to the center of the footing.

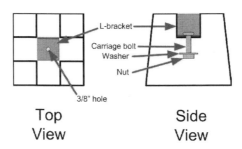

Top   Side
View   View

Figure 38 - Anchor L-Bracket

Level the Site

1. Your collector site should be at least 94" by 48".
2. Remove all grass and weeds from this site.
3. Level the ground of the entire site.

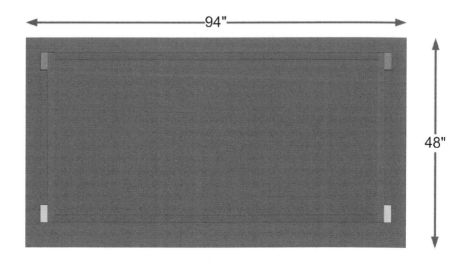

Figure 39 - Level the Area Around the Collector Site

Set the Footings

NOTE: The footings described below are just one possible example. Footing requirements vary widely by location (frost depth, wind conditions, etc.). Check with your local building department to assure compliance with regulatory prerequisites.

1. Place the frame on the cleared and level site.
2. Square the frame on the site.
3. Using string and wood stakes mark the corners where the notches touch the ground.

Figure 40 - Mark the Position for the Footings

4. Remove the string from the stakes.
5. Carefully remove the frame without disturbing the stakes.
6. Replace the string on the stakes.
7. Dig out the ground putting the corners of the footings at the positions of the string with the L-brackets facing out (against the short side).
8. Level the footings front-to-back and side-to-side.
9. Test fit the frame on top of the footings.
10. Adjust as necessary.
11. Backfill the footings into the ground.
12. Set the frame on the footings.

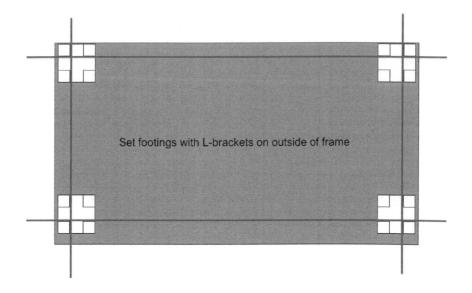

Set footings with L-brackets on outside of frame

Figure 41 - Check Footing Locations

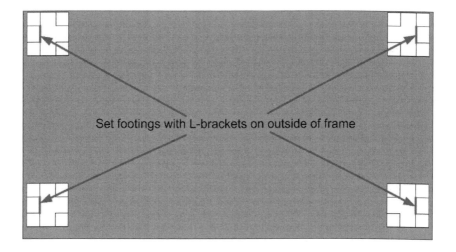

Set footings with L-brackets on outside of frame

Figure 42 - Assure Brackets Face Out

Set the Frame

1. Remove the string and the stakes.
2. Set the frame onto the footings.

3. Make sure that the entire frame is evenly seated on the footings and properly leveled.
4. Pre-drill ¼" holes through the L-bracket holes into the frame.
5. Bolt the L-brackets to the frame.

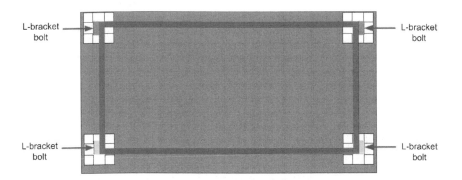

L-bracket bolt

L-bracket bolt

L-bracket bolt

L-bracket bolt

Figure 43 - Set the Frame on the Footings

Set the Collector

1. Pre-drill ½" clear holes at the top of the vertical boards A and C for the lag bolts (both sides).
2. Temporarily set the collector into place on the frame. Use nails to keep it in position for the next step.
3. Pre-drill ¼" pilot holes into the collector frame for the lag bolts so as not to split the wood of the collector.
4. Bolt the collector to the frame.
5. Remove the temporary nails.

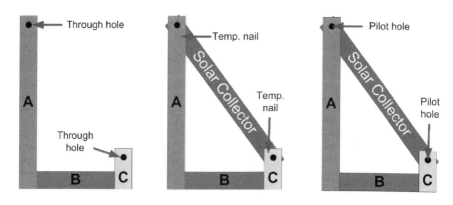

Figure 44 - Mount the Collector on the Frame

Install Ground Cover

Add decorative rock in front of the frame to keep mud from splashing on it. Do not allow plants, weeds, or tall grass to grow in front of your frame.

Part 3 Summary

Setting the proper angle of your solar collector toward the sun means tilting it slightly more towards the horizon than your latitude. Doing so increases the efficiency during the winter and decreases it in the summer.

Installing the frame on firm footings is essential to assure long, reliable service. Attaching the collector to the frame with lag bolts allows you to easily maintain or adjust the collector as needed.

Part 4 – Hook Up the Collector

The fluid used in the collector is automotive anti-freeze (ethylene glycol). You can also use peanut oil as a fluid but it requires fabricating metal lines rather than using flexible rubber hoses. Whatever fluid you choose, both will work well and both will not freeze.

In this part, you will route connection lines from the heat exchanger to the collector making sure that these lines gradually run uphill the entire way from the collector to the heat exchanger.

Connect the Expansion Tank

1. Position the expansion tank near the heat exchanger.
2. Attach it to a support with pipe strapping.
3. Fabricate a ¾" line to the top threaded connection of the heat exchanger.
4. Connect a threaded adapter to the end of the fabrication as shown at the right.

NOTE: The expansion tank is on the side that connects to the solar collector, not to the water heater.

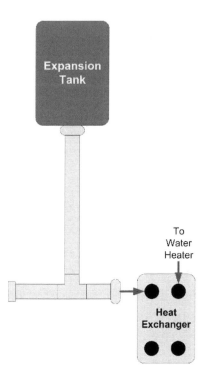

Figure 45 - Add the Expansion Tank to the Solar-Side Plumbing

Connect the Lines to the Heat Exchanger

NOTE: If you could not locate your solar collector below your water heater, see <u>Appendix A</u> for additional steps required at this point.

1. Connect two ¾" braided flex hoses to the two ¾" threaded exit stubs on the solar collector.
2. Connect two ¾" braided flex hoses to the two unused ¾" threaded connections on the heat exchanger.
3. Starting at the heat exchanger, fabricate ¾" copper lines routing these lines to the solar collector in as short and most direct route as possible. Do not solder them into place until the entire route is completed.
4. Mount the lines away from walls using 2x4 wood blocks to support them and stand them off from walls, floors, and ceilings.

5. Connect the HOT OUT line from the solar collector to the top threaded connection on the heat exchanger.

6. Connect the COLD IN line from the solar collector to the bottom threaded connection on the heat exchanger.

7. Once all lines are fabricated, disassemble them a few pieces at a time, sand, flux, and solder them together making sure that the proper angles are maintained.

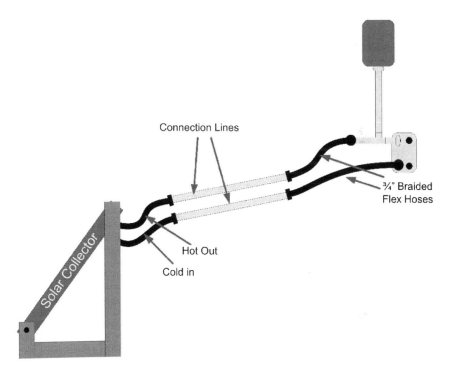

Connection Lines

¾" Braided Flex Hoses

Hot Out

Cold in

Solar Collector

Figure 46 - Connect the Solar Collector to the Heat Exchanger and Expansion Tank

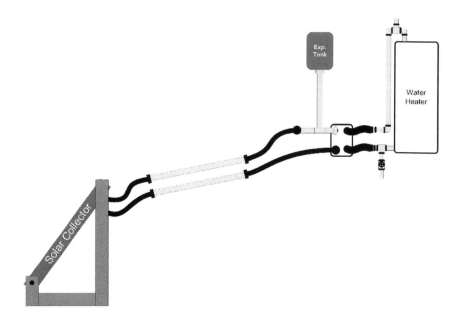

Figure 47 - Completed Assembly

Charge the System

1. Remove the expansion tank.
2. Through the mounting hole, slowly fill the line with the fluid trying to avoid putting air into the system as you pour. The more air you add now, the longer it will take to remove it later. This should take at about two to three gallons of fluid to completely top off the system, depending on how long your lines are.
3. Fill the system to about two inches from the top being careful not to overfill. There must be some air at the top of this pipe to allow proper operation of the expansion tank.
4. Put the expansion tank back on.
5. Wait one full day.
6. Check for leaks in the lines between the heat exchanger and the solar collector. If there are leaks, you must drain the fluid from these lines and repair them as needed. You do not need to drain the zigzag assembly in the solar collector (unless a leak occurs there).

7. Before the sun comes up on the next day (that is when the system is fully cooled to at least the temperature of the previous morning), remove the expansion tank and fill the line again to within two inches of the top (as before).
8. Put the expansion tank back on.
9. Wait one full day.
10. Repeat the level checking test until the fluid level stabilizes.

Insulate the Lines

1. Once you are certain that there are no leaks, use the Reflectix insulation to wrap all lines and fittings.
2. Wrap at least two layers of insulation on all lines in the house.
3. Wrap an additional layer of insulation on the outside lines between the house and the solar collector.
4. Caulk any holes to the house with expanding foam.

Part 4 Summary

Filling the collector lines with ethylene glycol fluid provides an efficient and safe way to transfer the heat from the solar collector to the heat exchanger. Check for leaks several times during the filling and charging process. Make sure that there is at least two inches of air in the top of the fill pipe so proper operation of the expansion tank can be maintained. Once you are certain there are no leaks, put at least two layers of Reflectix insulation on all inside pipes and at least three layers on all outside pipes. Check the fluid level about once a month on cool mornings always allowing at least two inches of air in the fill pipe.

It may take some time to "burp" all of the air out of your solar collector depending on how much air is suspended and dissolves in the fluid when you added it. Remember that this thin fluid will expand very quickly once the sun hits the collector. Do not check the fluid level when the collector is in the sun or when the system is hot.

⚠ **WARNING**: After installing this solar hot water collector into your home hot water system, the water temperature in your water heater will vary widely depending on how much sun is available each day. As a result, **the water temperature in your water heater will not be constant**.

Under certain conditions it is possible for scalding temperatures to be reached inside of the water heater.

To prevent scalding or burns <u>always assure proper cold-water mix</u> before showering, bathing, washing, or exposing skin to hot water.

NOTE: If your collector is too efficient and gets your water too hot, block part of it off with a tarp or board.

Appendix A – Parts List

The following is a pick list of parts available through your local Lowes big-box hardware stores. Prices are quoted from a Lowe's® hardware store in central Florida (less tax) as of 4-5-2009; your actual purchase price may vary. Small hardware (screws, washers, nuts, etc.) are not listed. If your water heater is a long distance from your solar collector, additional ¾" copper pipe, fittings and other miscellaneous parts will be needed (see also Appendix C regarding thermo-siphoning issues). I recommend finding a used patio door (tempered glass, not low-e glass) by posting a wanted ad on Craig's List (www.craigslist.com).

Qty	Description	Product UPC	P/N	Cost
1	6' Dual-pane fixed panel of patio door with frame **NOT LOW-E glass**	121966		$220.00
1	roll Reflectix® insulation 48" width	0716511340015	13358	$49.83
1	roll 2½" wide HVAC foil tape	0040074021792	237724	$15.98
12	¾"x10' copper pipe Type M	0720128020093	23791	$119.40
12	¾" copper pipe, street elbow (M-F)	0039923314086	21627	$23.40
2	¾" copper pipe, F-F elbow, 10-pack	0039923001832	11298	$17.84
4	¾" copper pipe, male threaded adapter	0039923037428	21850	$13.48
1	roll Teflon Tape, 12" x 520"	0046224255000	25010	$0.97
1	2 gallon expansion tank	0000013445272	160654	$49.00
4	¾" x 20"Female braided Water Heater hoses	0048643050105	25205	$35.52
2	5/4"x6"x8' pressure treated decking board	0717063556800	21210	$9.94
2	4'x8'x½" sheets of foil-backed insulating foam board	0719968210016	15328	$23.48
1	4'x8'x½" sheet of pressure treated plywood	0717063202769	202760	$24.97
3	2"x2"x8' pressure treated wood	0090489021702	204231	$5.94
2	cans High-temperature black	0020066163563	303288	$20.31

Qty	Description	Product UPC	P/N	Cost
	spray paint			
1	Exterior wood glue, waterproof	0051527949105	100575	$4.64
1	box Exterior Deck Screws, 2½" stainless steel	0764666528499	18284	$25.64
1	tube Micro Rain Gutter Sealing Caulk	0028756993056	224065	$4.97
1	can Expanding foam insulation, Great Stuff	0074985000119	13617	$3.48
1	roll ¼"x½" wide x 25' self-adhesive foam-rubber seal	0043374022797	66674	$3.14
4	2"x4"x8' pressure treated wood	0090489016760	46905	$11.88
4	Concrete Footings, Handi Block	0890248002009	53770	$35.92
4	Exterior L-brackets	0044315044823	63162	$8.92
4	3/8" x 3" exterior lag screws	0008236085259	63357	$2.00
1	can Acetone	0023857724417	206558	$6.98
2	Silver Solder Kits	0716447924938	98978	$38.96
1	¾" 2-hole copper pipe U-strap, 25-pack	0039923002679	301311	$12.65
1	Stainless Steel Heat Exchanger (30 plate minimum)	eBay®	eBay	$88.00
				$657.24

Total with $10 used door: $447.44

Total with $220 new door: $657.24

Figure 48 - Parts List

Appendix B – Timer Option

To further improve the efficiency of your new solar hot water system, you can add a timer to an electric water heater that turns the normal heating elements ON only at certain times of the day. Such timers are readily available at home construction retailers and should only be installed by a certified electrician.

Figure 49 - Intermatic® WH40 and EH40 240V Water Heater Timers

When using such a timer in conjunction with the solar collector, I suggest turning ON the heating elements for two hours just after the time when the sun no longer contributes to the heating of water. This assures you hot water on sunless days warmed to the minimum temperature you already enjoy.

For example, if the sun on collector no longer contributes to heating the water at 2:00 P.M., set this timer to turn ON at 2:30 P.M. and turn off at 4:30 P.M.

Remember that when using hot water in a timer optioned system, the water in the water heater is always heated to its normal temperature at the time when the timer turns off (here, 4:30 P.M.). After this time, the stored heat in the water heater slowly dissipates based on how well the water heater is insulated. The water inside the water heater then gets reheated the next day when the sun contributes to the heating of the water. Changes in your use of hot water may be needed to be adjusted to assure the availability of the hottest water. Heavy early morning usage can be changed to late afternoon thereby assuring availability of hot water. Schedules for clothes washing, showers, and the like may need to be staggered based on the availability of the amount of hot water stored in your water heater.

If heavy morning usage is unavoidable, also set the timer to turn on and off for a brief time early in the morning (say 3:00-3:30 A.M.).

Appendix C – Circulation Pumps

There are times when thermo-siphoning between the collector panel and the water heater will not work. It is more frugal to try your system using the thermo-siphon principle first but plan to add circulation pumps if needed. With this approach, if the results are satisfactory, you have not made an unnecessary expense. But when the harvested heat is not transferred to the water heater with thermo-siphoning, low-power circulation pumps can help to assist fluid flow.

An elegant solution for inadequate thermo-siphoning is to use a 12 Volt photovoltaic panel as a power source and two small 12 Volt circulation pumps. In this approach, the pumps only run when there is adequate sunlight and turn off automatically during cloudy days and at night. When there is not enough sunlight to create electricity, there is also not enough sunlight to heat the water so the system is relatively self regulating by the position of the solar panel.

Important: Make sure that all local low-voltage electrical codes, building permits, and necessary inspections are complied with in your solar panel and pump installation.

Inline Oil/Anti-Freeze Circulation Pump

A solar-powered inline fluid circulation pump helps move the heated oil or anti-freeze from the solar collector to the heat exchanger. Since the collector fluid can potentially be very hot, normal fluid pumps will most likely not work because of their limited operating temperatures (check the operating temperature range before buying any pump). A good type of pump to use in these conditions is a gear-driven automotive-style oil scavenge pump. A small 12V electric scavenge pump (such as those used for moving hot oil in turbo charged motorcycles) is available from GK Wholesale, 5 Maplecrest Lane, Colts Neck, NJ 07722 (see http://myworld.ebay.com/ebaymotors/gkwholesale/?_trksid=p4340.l2559)

Figure 50 - A Low-Power, High-Temperature Fluid Circulation Pump

Inline Water Circulation Pump

A solar-powered inline hot-water circulation pump helps circulate the harvested heat from the heat exchanger into the water heater. Since the heat exchanger temperature can be potentially very hot, normal water pumps will most likely not work because of their limited operating temperatures (check the operating temperature range before buying your pump). A good type of pump to use in these conditions is a home heating water circulation pump but most are not efficient enough to be run from a photovoltaic solar panel. The EL-SID 12V high-efficiency electric hot water circulation pump is manufactured by Ivan Labs, 305 Circle W, Jupiter, FL 33458 and available from many online retailers (search for **El Sid Pump**).

Figure 51 - A Low-Power, High-Temperature Water Circulation Pump

Photovoltaic Solar Panel

A 12V photovoltaic solar panel can create free electricity to run your pumps. Panel output depends entirely on the pumps you choose. Using the recommended pumps listed above requires a 12 Volt 55-85 Watt photovoltaic panel (longer runs need the bigger 85 Watt panel). Good companion, well-made, cost-effective solar panels are available from UL Solar, 3805 S. Jones Blvd., Las Vegas, NV 89146 (see http://www.ul-solar.com/). Their 55 Watt model is number STP055P and their 80 Watt model is number STP085P.

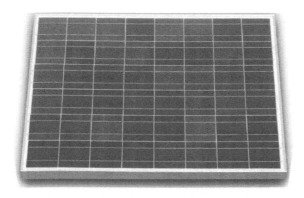

Figure 52 - A Typical 12V Solar Panel

Installation

Install the pumps in series with the cold fluid lines (see Figure 53 and Figure 54). For the fluid pump, you will need to add another short piece of ¾" braided flex hose between the pump and the solar collector (if using peanut oil instead of antifreeze, you will need another metal fabricated line).

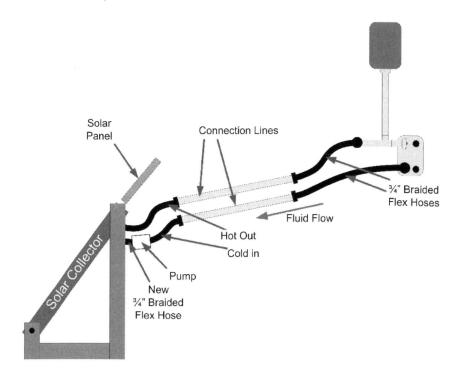

Figure 53 - Inline Fluid Circulation Pump

On the water heater, install the pump on the cold water side. You will need to add another short piece of ¾" braided flex hose between the pump and the water heater.

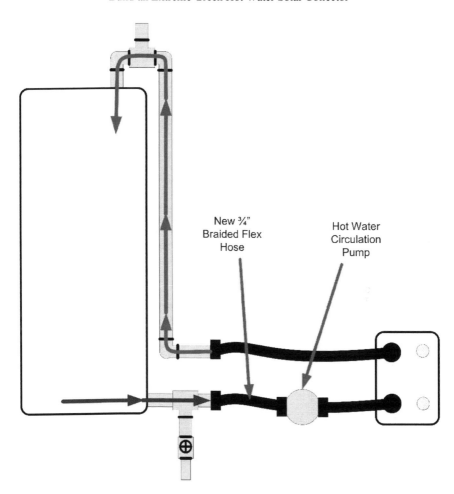

New ¾"
Braided Flex
Hose

Hot Water
Circulation
Pump

Figure 54 - Inline Water Circulation Pump

Mount this pump in such a position that in the event of a water leak the pump will not become submerged or wet.

Fabricate a solid mount on which each pump will sit and attach one to the back panel of the solar collector and the other at a convenient location near the heat exchanger.

Connect weatherproof wires from the two pumps directly to the solar panel (+ to + and – to –). Run the wires from the water heater pump to the solar panel along the same route as the connecting lines. It is a good idea to add a 2,200 micro-farad 50 Volt electrolytic capacitors (available from <u>Radio Shack</u>) at close to each circulation pump to help stabilize the voltage. Connect the+ lead of the capacitor to the + wire and the – lead to the – wire (see Figure 55).

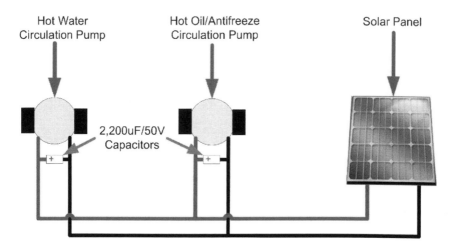

Figure 55 - Add Capacitors at the Pumps

Position the solar panel in such a way that it stops producing electricity once the sun moves to a position where heat is no longer harvested by the collector.

Figure 56 - System with Photovoltaic Panel

An optional Universal Side of Pole mounting kit is also available from UL Solar, 3805 S. Jones Blvd., Las Vegas, NV 89146 (see http://www.ul-solar.com/).

Figure 57 - A Sample Mounting Pole

Appendix D – Troubleshooting

As it is with all human designs, sometimes your best laid plans just cannot anticipate every possible obstacle or issue. Don't feel alone in such matters; recent history documents a great number of huge faux pas committed by the finest (and highest-paid) minds on the face of the planet. You may have just joined this elite group. Alexander Pope summed it up well in his famous quote: *To err is human...* and I have yet to meet a non-human.

Aside from regular glass cleaning and grass trimming, your hot water solar collector should be reasonably maintenance free (mine has been running for over five years without as much as a hiccup). However, the sun if nothing else is relentless and given enough time it can cause fading of collector paint, leaking of insulation seals on the double-pane glass panel, leaking of soldered connections, and blistering of reflective insulation inside of the collector. If you have painted your collector box, annually check for weathering of the paint and repaint or repair as needed. Check your system for leaks at least once a month (daily at a minimum after first installing it) and always maintain your system to assure peak performance.

Sediment collecting in the bottom of your water heater is the main problem you will face. Sediment comes from a variety of places like dirt in your water supply line, minerals in a hard water source, or normal deterioration of the internal surfaces of your water heater. If you are using an electric water heater as a backup/storage system, normal heating element degradation can also result in sediment in the bottom of the tank. Regardless of the source of sediment, it can accumulate and eventually block the circulation through the heat exchanger circuit. Normal maintenance in any water heater is to rinse and flush sediment from the bottom of the tank each year. Normal maintenance on electric water heaters also includes routinely checking and replacing the sacrificial anode. Refer to your water heater manufacturer's website for information on recommended maintenance for your particular brand of water heater and always follow their maintenance recommendations.

At a minimum, annually back-flushing the heat-exchanger circuit is also recommended since this same sediment that accumulates inside of your water heater can also migrate into and plug up this circuit. If you cannot free the sediment or internal obstructions from the heat exchanger, you will most likely need to replace it.

Below are some of the most common issues and typical solutions for a solar hot water system.

Symptom	Cause	Solutions
Insulation inside the collector is sagging	Poor support of insulation	Reattach insulation with additional support
	Heat build-up in collector	Add a circulation pump to help dissipate heat quicker (see Appendix C)
Water inside bottom of collector	Leak	Check seals on glass panel. Check seams on box corners and bottom plywood.
Fog inside collector	Leak	Check seals on glass panel. Check seams on box corners and bottom plywood.
Oil/anti-freeze inside collector	Bad solder joint	Drain and pressure test zigzag assembly. Locate leak and re-solder joint. Check by pressure testing. Allow zigzag assembly to dry completely before refilling (remove all moisture from lines).
Collector or pipe smells	Leaky fitting	Check for bad gasket on fitting connections. Properly tighten all fitting connections (do not over tighten and crush gaskets).

Symptom	Cause	Solutions
	Bad solder joint	Drain and pressure test zigzag assembly and associated plumbing. Locate leak and re-solder joint. Check by pressure testing. Allow zigzag assembly and plumbing to dry completely before refilling (remove all moisture from lines).
Water is very hot but only for a few minutes	Inadequate thermo-siphoning	Add pumps to your system (see Appendix C)
Collector pipes get extremely hot	Inadequate thermo-siphoning	Add pumps to your system (see Appendix C)
System used to work fine but hot water output has dropped or totally stopped	Weather change	Supplement heat with a timer (see Appendix B)
	Dirty glass	Clean the glass
	Collector shaded during prime sun time	Trim obstructive branches to permit longer sun exposure on collector.
	Low fluid level in collector	Trapped air has finally "burped" from the zigzag assembly resulting in low fluid level. Refill with oil/anti-freeze as per your system design on a cool morning before the sun comes up.
	Drip in hot water faucet	Repair or replace leaky faucet

Symptom	Cause	Solutions
	Change in hot water consumption	Your use of hot water has grown from your original design. Add a larger water heater and more collectors as required. Supplement with a timer (see <u>Appendix B</u>).
	Change in daily use	Your daily use of hot water has changed. Monitor hot water use (clothes washing, dish washing, bathing times, etc.) to see if several coincide. If so, try to stagger days on which use is better balanced. Supplement with a timer (see <u>Appendix B</u>).
	Debris or obstructions in heat exchanger or pipes	Back-flush heat exchanger to remove deposits. Flush water heater to remove deposits (if water heater is old/defective, replace the water heater). If problem persists, test the calcium level in your water (may be necessary to add a water softener).
System does not produce enough hot water	Drip in hot water faucet	Repair or replace leaky faucet
	Inadequate thermo-siphoning	(Usually has another symptom of very hot water for a short period of time). Add pumps to your system (see <u>Appendix C</u>).

Symptom	Cause	Solutions
	Collector design is inadequate	One good way to test your system's hot-water production ability is to turn off the water heater. If you notice after a few days that the system cannot keep up with your demand, the collector size is too small. Add a timer (see Appendix B) or add more collectors.

Appendix E – Tropical Climates

In tropical climates where there is **absolutely no chance of freezing**, the heat exchanger can be eliminated from the circuit and the water heated directly from the solar collector. In such a configuration, system efficiency is increased and costs are reduced considerably (no heat exchanger, expansion tank, or peanut oil required).

However, there is no such thing as a free lunch and there are hidden risks associated with a direct connection between the water heater and the solar collector. Here, the full pressure of your water supply will be applied to the soldered connections you made in the solar hot water collector and the hoses, pipes, and fittings of the connecting circuit thereby increasing the potential for system leaks. If you live in an area where pressure transients or pressure surges in your water system are experienced, this also increases the chances for anomalous system leaks. Because of this increased risk you should routinely verify that your system is not leaking (at least weekly).

See the drawing below for connects in the Convection System (see also Figure 47 for comparison).

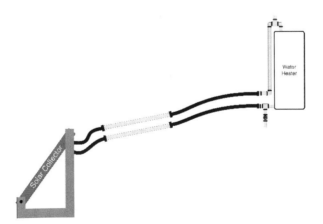

Figure 58 - Direct Connection of the Solar Collector to the Water Heater, Convection System

See the drawing below for connects in the Pump-assisted System (see also Figure 52 and Figure 53 for comparison). Note that the oil pump is not required.

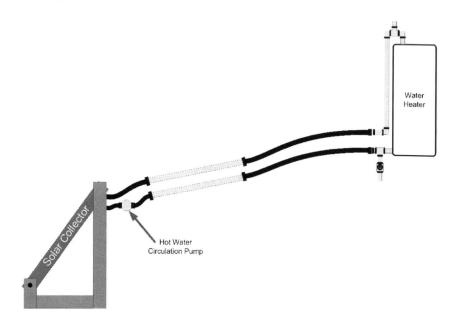

Water
Heater

Solar Collector

Hot Water
Circulation Pump

Figure 59 - Direct Connection of the Solar Collector to the Water Heater, Pump-assisted System

ABOUT THE AUTHOR

Hailing from a small blue-collar town in Wisconsin, I lived next door to my loving Czechoslovakian grandparents for the first 12 years of my life. As a child, I was attracted to the fascinating physical aspects of the world, trying to figure out why things were as they are (or seem). While in college, I found I could discuss complicated concepts with others in everyday language. Combining this ability with my intense curiosity and an attraction to technology, I became a technical writer for Bell Telephone Laboratories (Bell Labs), the inventors of the transistor.

College was briefly interrupted by the Vietnam War. I was in the Air Force when I met and married my wife. She taught me how to appreciate the non-technical side of life, finding value in diversity. I found our young relationship stressful and stumbled through the early years of our marriage. But my wife looked at our challenges differently and engaged herself in a life-long self-improvement quest to better understand herself, her personal spirituality, and find her true path. I grew as she did.

The insights I learned along this challenging life journey profoundly changed me mentally, emotionally, and spiritually. I now search for the meaning to life from within. I feel a personal responsibility to the earth like the immortal words of Robert Baden-Powell, founder of the Boy Scouts: *Try and leave this world a little better than you found it.*

I find myself today performing similar tasks to those of ancient translators, that is, to write down in simple, everyday terms the workings of complicated things. The guides I write hopefully help us all walk more softly on the earth and leave it a better place for future generations.

This guide is one in a series of do-it-yourself projects that can help you not only lower your energy usage but also create a statement about your higher consciousness to future generations. R. Buckminster Fuller said in 1968, "Now there is one outstandingly important fact regarding Spaceship Earth, and that is that no instruction book came with it." Hopefully, this guide can help fill one small part this missing need.

Other titles available at Amazon.com by Philip Rastocny include:

- Althea: A Story of Love
- Meditation for Geeks (and other left-brained people)
- Build an Extreme Green™ Raised Bed Garden
- Build an Extreme Green Rain Barrel
- Extreme Green Organic Gardening
- Extreme Green Organic Gardening 2012
- Build an Extreme Green Composter
- Build and Extreme Green Hot Water Solar Collector
- Build an Extreme Green Squirrel-Proof Bird Feeder
- The Extreme Green Guide to Wind Turbines
- The Extreme Green Guide to Solar Electricity
- The Extreme Green Guide to Improving Mileage
- The Extreme Green Appliance Buying Guide
- Extreme Audio 1: House Wiring
- Extreme Audio 2: Line Filtering
- Extreme Audio 3: Chassis Leakage
- Extreme Audio 4: Interconnect Cables
- Extreme Audio 5: Speaker Wires

BRadley Street
Trigg Street (458 Trigg St.)

Carol Wood
Thursday @ 10:30
458 Trigg Street

Made in the USA
Columbia, SC
02 March 2021